Psyche and Eros

Marcia Williams

CAMBRIDGE
UNIVERSITY PRESS

Zeus,
chief god

Zeus's eagle

Aphrodite,
goddess of love,
daughter of Zeus

Mount Olympus,
home of the gods

Eros,
god of love, son of Aphrodite

Hermes,
messenger of the gods, son of Zeus

Psyche, a mortal so beautiful that Aphrodite grew jealous of her

Psyche's worried parents

Psyche's troublesome sisters

Pleasure, daughter of Psyche and Eros

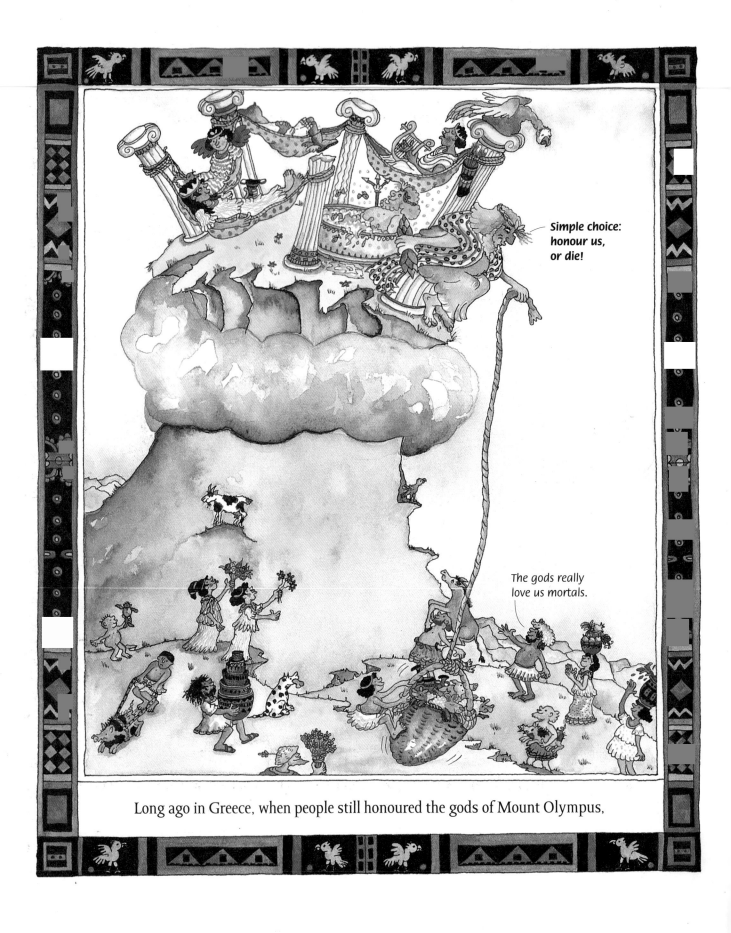

Long ago in Greece, when people still honoured the gods of Mount Olympus,

a mortal king and queen had three beautiful daughters.
The loveliest by far was Psyche, the youngest.

Greeks travelled from far and wide to gaze upon Psyche's beauty. Psyche was so perfect that many people believed she must really be Aphrodite, the goddess of love.

When Aphrodite heard that she was being compared to a mortal, her rage shook Mount Olympus.

Overcome by anger, Aphrodite sent her son, Eros, to punish the unfortunate Psyche.

Eros was an archer, whose arrows had magic golden tips that could make anyone, mortal or immortal, fall in love with the next person they saw.

Aphrodite told Eros to pierce Psyche with one of his arrows and cause her to fall in love with a worthless rogue.

Eros flew down from Olympus, ready to do his mother's bidding.

When Eros saw Psyche, he was so startled by her beauty that he accidentally pierced himself with one of his arrows.

And so, unbeknown to Psyche, he fell in love with her.

Meanwhile, Psyche's father was growing worried about his youngest daughter, for both her sisters were now married to fine princes.

Yet Psyche had no suitors. Her father suspected it was because she had angered Aphrodite. He decided to consult a priestess.

The priestess could foretell the will of the gods. Her words terrified Psyche's parents, but they dared not disobey the priestess for fear of a worse disaster befalling them.

So the next night, as instructed by the priestess, Psyche was dressed in a wedding gown, led to a lonely rock on the summit of a high mountain, and left there all on her own.

Her parents ran back quickly to the safety of their home.

Psyche sat on the rock, shaking with fear, for it had been foretold that a winged foe would claim her as his bride. Terrified, Psyche imagined every sort of monster dragging her off the rock.

What a windy monster.

But it was no winged demon that lifted Psyche up, it was Zephyrus, the gentle West Wind. Zephyrus carried Psyche carefully down the mountain.

He laid her down in a far-off valley, where she slept until dawn.

In the morning light, Psyche saw before her a glittering golden palace with its burnished doors wide open.

Nervously, Psyche entered the hall. Although she could see no-one, she could hear the murmur of welcoming voices.

Psyche wandered from room to room, amazed at the richness of her surroundings. She came at last to a room where the table was laid ready for a feast.

Feeling hungry, Psyche seated herself on the only chair. To her amazement, invisible hands began to serve her with dishes of exotic food, while sweet voices sang to the music of a lyre played by unseen fingers.

Psyche was tired from her many strange experiences and, after eating her fill, found a bed on which to sleep.

When Psyche awoke, night had fallen and she could see only shadows and silhouettes.

She heard a sudden rush of wings entering the window and cried out, sure that the monster was about to claim her.

But the hand that took hers was gentle and the voice that spoke to her was kind.
The strange, shadowy figure asked Psyche to consent to be his wife and
live forever in the beautiful palace.
During the day, the invisible hand-maidens would care for Psyche,
and at night he would visit her.

The only condition was that Psyche should never try to look upon his face.

Psyche agreed, and for many weeks she lived contentedly. Her new husband proved kind and had a store of amusing stories.

But gradually, Psyche grew lonely for her sisters, for invisible hand-maidens are not good company.

Psyche implored her husband to allow her to see her sisters. Reluctantly he agreed, but warned Psyche not to let her sisters persuade her to look upon his face as that would be the end of their happiness.

The next day, Zephyrus blew Psyche's sisters into the valley.

They begged to meet Psyche's rich husband and provider.

The sisters nagged at Psyche until Zephyrus blew them both home.

Before long, Psyche began to feel lonely again. Once more, she begged to see her sisters.

Her husband agreed, but repeated his warning to Psyche that she must not let her sisters tempt her into looking upon his face.

Zephyrus gently wafted the sisters to the secret valley. Psyche was delighted, but her sisters were jealous of her good fortune. They pestered Psyche into admitting that she had never seen her husband.

Hoping to acquire some of Psyche's wealth for themselves, they convinced her that her husband was a monster waiting to eat her. The sisters persuaded Psyche to kill her husband that very night.

Psyche was frightened and confused. That night, as her husband lay asleep, she lit the lamp.

Taking up the knife, Psyche looked down at her sleeping husband. Here was no greedy, scaly monster.

It was the handsome god, Eros, who, having fallen so in love with Psyche, had devised this secret way of being with a mortal.

As Psyche hastily put down the knife, she pricked her hand on one of Eros's magic golden arrows.

As a result, when she turned again to look at Eros, she fell instantly in love with him.

Trembling at the thought that she might have killed him, Psyche accidentally spilt hot oil from her lamp onto Eros.

Opening his eyes with a start, Eros beheld the beautiful Psyche staring down at him.

Reproachfully, Eros kissed Psyche's quivering hand, then he flew out of the window and into the night.

As Eros vanished among the stars, the glittering palace melted away like a snowflake. Sad Psyche found herself alone once more on the barren mountain summit.

Devastated at having lost Eros, Psyche threw herself into a river that gushed down the mountain.

But the river, unwilling to drown the sweetheart of Eros, carried Psyche to safety.

So Psyche determined to go in search of Eros and find some way of winning him back.

She prayed to the gods to help her but, fearing Aphrodite's wrath, they all turned a deaf ear to her pleas.

Psyche even prayed to Aphrodite, believing remorse would soften the goddess's heart.

But Aphrodite was still jealous of Psyche's beauty and was enraged that Eros had fallen in love with a mortal.

Hoping to rid herself of Psyche once and for all, Aphrodite set her a series of seemingly impossible tasks.

First, Aphrodite pointed to a huge pile of mixed grain with which she fed the doves that pulled her chariot. She told Psyche that, before nightfall, she must separate the various types, grain by grain.

It was already noon and Psyche felt it was a hopeless task. But, for the love of Eros, she resolved to try.

Minute piles of wheat, barley, millet and other grains started to form.

But the hours were passing and the vast pile of mixed grain seemed to grow no smaller . . .

. . . until a colony of ants who had been watching Psyche offered their help.
Tiny as the ants were, they moved with the speed of lightning, carrying grain
several times their size.

When nightfall came, Aphrodite returned to mock Psyche's failure.

She found all the grain sorted into neat piles.

Aphrodite was not pleased with Psyche's success.
Furiously, she thought up an even harder task to set Psyche.

The next morning, Aphrodite pointed to a flock of golden, man-eating sheep on the far side of a river. The goddess told Psyche that if she wanted to see Eros again, she must fetch her some wool from the sheep.

Brave Psyche prepared to wade across the river to fetch the wool, but the reeds held her back. They whispered to her to wait until late afternoon when the river had lulled the sheep to sleep.

Psyche sat by the river and watched the fierce flock. The sheep growled and grunted at each other, sniffing the air in the hope of catching the scent of some unfortunate human victim.

All day, the river kept up a steady murmuring and, as the sun began to drop in the sky,
one by one the bloodthirsty sheep closed their eyes and lay down to sleep.

Psyche crossed the river and stealthily, without waking a single sheep, she gathered
up the wool caught in the grass and on the bushes until her arms were full.

That night, Aphrodite threw the wool into the air in her rage at Psyche's victory.
Then the goddess divulged to Psyche a task that she was sure would be the
death of this annoying mortal.

Aphrodite gave Psyche a small jug and told her to fill it at the Fountain of Forgetfulness.

The fountain was high up in the mountains, where no mortal ever ventured.

Psyche, still hoping to win Eros back, took the jug and set off up the steep cliff.

Up and up she climbed until she could hear the water gushing from the rocks.

Just as Psyche began to think that she might succeed, two vast dragons, who guarded the fountain, roared out of a cave, engulfing Psyche in their fiery breath.

Zeus's eagle, who was friends with Eros and owed him a favour, had been watching Psyche struggle up the cliff.

The eagle now flew to her aid. Taking the jug from Psyche, he filled it for her at the icy fountain.

Psyche, her goal achieved, hastily retreated from the dragons' wrath. She climbed happily back down the mountain, convinced that Aphrodite would now relent and let her return to Eros.

But Aphrodite was now determined to send Psyche to her death. She gave Psyche a box to take to the Underworld, telling her that she must ask the goddess Persephone to part with a little of her beauty.

At the thought of visiting the Underworld, Psyche's nerve failed her. Instead, she climbed a tall tower.

In despair, she prepared to jump to her death. But the tower whispered helpful advice to Psyche.

Following the tower's directions, brave Psyche set off down a dark chasm, and then along a thorn-tangled path. In her mouth, Psyche carried two coins and in each hand she held a honey cake.

Warned by the tower not to give up the cakes or the money until the right moment, Psyche ignored the lame man who asked for help.

Psyche also ignored the pleas of three women who wanted help with their weaving.

When Psyche reached the River Styx, which must be crossed to reach the Underworld, she ignored the help offered by a floating corpse, but she let Charon, the ferryman, ferry her across the river and take a coin from her, as the tower had advised.

Eventually, Psyche reached the gates of Persephone's palace. These were guarded by the dog, Cerberus.

Cerberus loved eating humans, but Psyche threw him a cake and slipped by as his three heads fought for it.

Cautioned by the tower not to sit or eat, Psyche promptly begged Persephone for a small part of her beauty for Aphrodite. Impressed by Psyche's bravery, Persephone willingly obliged.

Psyche set off to return the way she had come. On the way, she threw Cerberus the other honey cake . . .

and gave Charon the last coin.
At last, after many strange encounters with the spirits . . .

Psyche reached the Upperworld. Only then did she forget the tower's last warning, not to open the box.

Thinking that a tiny part of Persephone's beauty might help her win Eros back, Psyche lifted the lid.

But it wasn't beauty that stole from the box, it was a death-like sleep which overcame Psyche.

Luckily, Eros had now recovered from his oil burn and, unbeknown to Aphrodite, he was searching for Psyche.

Eros flew back and forth over the land looking for signs of his beloved Psyche,
until, at last, he caught sight of her sleeping figure far below,
half-hidden by a cloud of sleep.

Swooping downwards, Eros wafted the
sleep back into the box and closed the lid.

Immediately, Psyche awoke and the
delighted pair were reunited at last.

But, realising they still had to pacify the gods, Psyche then set off to return Aphrodite's box.

Eros went to plead with Zeus, the mightiest of all the gods, to approve his marriage to a mortal.

Zeus, who was known for his quick temper and readiness to hurl thunderbolts around, was in an unusually good mood and indulgently agreed to make Psyche immortal.

Hermes, the messenger of the gods, was sent to bring Psyche to Mount Olympus.

There, Psyche was given sacred nectar to drink from a golden cup.

As Psyche drank, two gossamer wings sprang from her shoulders, and so she became immortal and able to stay with Eros.

A magnificent wedding feast was held and all the gods joined in the celebrations. Apollo played his lyre so gaily that even Aphrodite forgot her anger and danced.

Eros never flew away from Psyche again, and when some time later a beautiful daughter was born to them, they called her Pleasure, and they all lived together, happily ever after.

Cambridge Reading

General Editors
Richard Brown and Kate Ruttle

Consultant Editor
Jean Glasberg

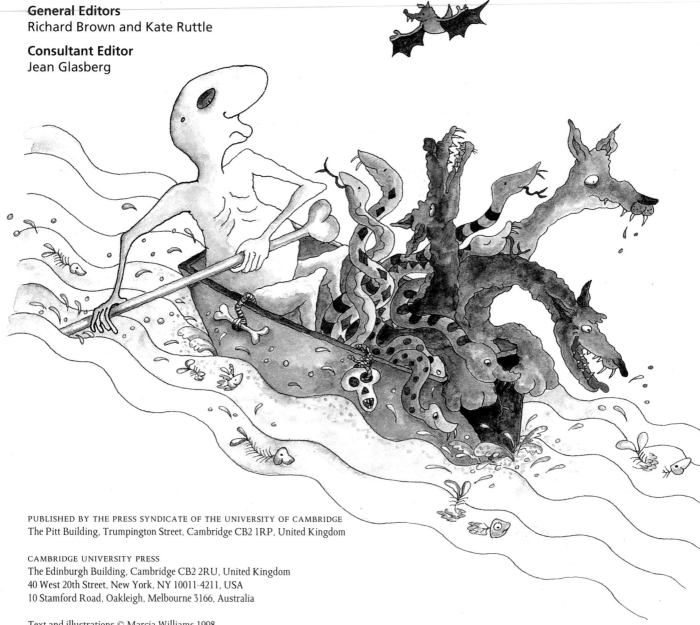

PUBLISHED BY THE PRESS SYNDICATE OF THE UNIVERSITY OF CAMBRIDGE
The Pitt Building, Trumpington Street, Cambridge CB2 1RP, United Kingdom

CAMBRIDGE UNIVERSITY PRESS
The Edinburgh Building, Cambridge CB2 2RU, United Kingdom
40 West 20th Street, New York, NY 10011-4211, USA
10 Stamford Road, Oakleigh, Melbourne 3166, Australia

First published 1998

Printed in the United Kingdom at the University Press, Cambridge

A catalogue record for this book is available from the British Library

ISBN 0 521 47786 7 paperback